Reimagine

There is Something More

ALINGA GODBER

This book is a work of non-fiction. Unless otherwise noted, the author and the publisher make no explicit guarantees as to the accuracy of the information contained in this book and in some cases, names of people and places have been altered to protect their privacy.

WestBow Press books may be ordered through booksellers or by contacting:

WestBow Press
A Division of Thomas Nelson & Zondervan
1663 Liberty Drive
Bloomington, IN 47403
www.westbowpress.com
844-714-3454

Author photo by Jessica Rock, Rock Photography.

ISBN: 978-1-6642-6628-5 (sc)
ISBN: 978-1-6642-6627-8 (e)

Print information available on the last page.

WestBow Press rev. date: 6/9/2022

Contents

Acknowledgments

Thank You Jesus!

Chapter 1
MY TESTIMONY

My story is common. Many people keep silent, ashamed to share with anyone how much they are suffering. Depression. Severe anxiety. Worry. Fear. Suicidal thoughts. Yes, that was me. I would act normally when around others, be cheerful and laugh, but there was utter chaos happening within.

I felt emotional heaviness at a very young age. I was withdrawn. I was teased by family, friends, and classmates all the way through my senior year in high school. That created insecurity and rejection, which led to me seeking relationships to try to fix the hurt and broken areas in my heart. I did not feel loved. I did what I could to distract myself from the negative feelings eating me up inside: get drunk, partake in drugs here and there, shop, work extra hours, binge watch television, and whatever else I could do to distract from the darkness in my mind. As the years went on, things got worse.

Finally, things got so bad that I found myself locked in my bathroom, sitting on the floor, hunched over, weeping out of control, and begging for God to help me. I felt like I was losing my mind. I couldn't escape it. My mind was in the darkest place it had ever been. I felt completely alone with no one to understand.

At that moment I felt like I wanted to end it all. Suddenly, I felt a prompting to get up and go to my bedroom, where the

Holy Spirit drew my eyes to a book that a friend had given me two years before. It was called *Victory Over the Darkness* by Neil T. Anderson. Through Jesus, this book started me on the road to freedom. For seven years, I wandered around the wilderness trying to find my way out, but I was never alone. Jesus was beside me, teaching me. I learned what it really meant to be a child of God and a follower of Jesus, and how Satan so cleverly deceived me. "Don't let anyone capture you with empty philosophies and high-sounding nonsense that come from human thinking and from the spiritual powers of this world, rather than from Christ" (Colossians 2:8).

My testimony is evidence of the confident hope we have in the promises of God through Jesus. Our testimonies are His testimonies. They are testimonies of His never-ending pursuit of us, and of His love, mercy, grace, and patience.

All the years I had spent going from church to church, seeking, searching, and digging for the precious stone I knew was there, were about to pay off. I had an image in my mind of this life with Jesus that I wasn't getting by attending church for two hours on a Sunday morning. I knew there was something more. There was a pulling at my heart to keep running after it. That "it" was Him. It was Jesus. God was calling me, and the Holy Spirit was guiding me. I left the path of destruction for the narrow road—no longer to walk as the rest of the world but to live the life God has placed before me. A year ago, I had a dream that I was in a conference room. There was a beautiful buffet with the brightest and most delicious food I had ever seen in my life. The room was full of people sitting in their chairs looking straight ahead. No one was at the buffet except me. I stood in front of the food with my plate, anticipating the experience my mouth was about to have with some very large shrimp. I looked around at everyone and wondered why they weren't eating this food that was freely provided for us. Then I woke up.

God has such an amazing array of revelatory food for us. We

are fed through His Word and through experiences with Him, which draw us closer and make us hungry for more. Just as with a physical buffet, people are eating different foods. Some are eating appetizers, others a hearty main course, and still others are having dessert. There are some foods that people do not like and choose not to eat or don't have very often. Regardless of what food someone eats, everyone is eating from the same buffet. For those in Christ, Jesus is our buffet—the Word of God. When we begin to feed our spirits, we become more sensitive to the voice of the Holy Spirit. We start to discern direction in prayer (who and what to pray for), we pray more in tongues, worship and praise become a more intimate experience with God, and dreams, visions, prophecy, and prophetic signs and symbols can become a regular part of each day.

As I mentioned before, some choose not to have certain items from the buffet. There are some who don't believe in praying in tongues or that God speaks to us in dreams. Many, even Christians, do not step up with their plate to taste and see all that God has for them. Some believers are happy they were invited to the meal, but then they just sit, satisfied being in the environment with others who are feasting on all that God has instead of tasting for themselves. I invite you to come on a journey to discover freedom, truth, and, if you so choose, a new and greater relationship with our Lord, Jesus Christ.

> Drink deeply of the pleasures of this God. Experience for yourself the joyous mercies he gives to all who turn to hide themselves in him. (Psalm 34:8 TPT)

> Live no longer as the Gentiles do, for they are hopelessly confused. Their minds are full of darkness; they wander far from the life God gives because they have closed their minds and

hardened their hearts against him. They have no sense of shame. They live for lustful pleasure and eagerly practice every kind of impurity. But that isn't what you learned about Christ. Since you have heard about Jesus and have learned the truth that comes from him, throw off your old sinful nature and your former way of life, which is corrupted by lust and deception. Instead, let the Spirit renew your thoughts and attitudes. Put on your new nature, created to be like God—truly righteous and holy. (Ephesians 4:17–24 NLT)

Chapter 2

THE GIFT, THE GARDEN, THE KINGDOM

Do you desire eternal life? It begins with a gift from God called salvation. It is the opportunity to be reunited with God since we have all been separated from Him because of sin. When we do the things that God has instructed us not to do, we sin. Salvation is the gift of eternal life through Jesus. You can exchange the burdens of this world for peace, love, and joy. God gave me a gift box. I accepted it, as many Christians or new believers do, but never closely examined the contents inside. This same gift is being offered to you. This book contains the instructions that were inside my box that led me to having amazing experiences with Jesus. If you choose to follow Jesus and these very simple instructions, you can have your own experience with Him. What God does for one, He will do for another. He does not favor one person above the next.

> Then Peter replied, "I see very clearly that God shows no favoritism." (Acts 10:34 NLT)

JESUS—THE SON OF GOD

Jesus is the Son of God. He is the visible image of God, who has always existed. He is the supreme being over all creation in heaven and on earth. There is none above Him. Everything that has been created was created through Him, and it is by Him that all of creation is held together (Colossians 1:15–17). When Adam and Eve sinned against God by disobeying Him, it caused a separation between God and humans. To cover their sin, God covered them with the skin of animals. Blood had to be shed to cover their sin. From that point forward, when anyone sinned (disobeyed the commands of God), the blood of a perfect bull or a lamb had to be shed to cover that sin in order for the person to be back in right standing with God. This practice was only a temporary fix. Humans could never remain in right standing with God due to the evil intent of our hearts.

> Then the Lord saw that the wickedness of man was great in the earth, and that every intent of the thoughts of his heart was only evil continually. (Genesis 6:5 NKJV)

Therefore, something permanent had to be done.

The purchase price for our sins is so high that no person would ever be able to pay it, so God intervened on our behalf, offering the payment for our offense, our rebellion against Him. Before the dawn of creation, it was God's selfless plan to sacrifice His perfect, spotless lamb, His son, Jesus. It was His love for the Father and His love for us that brought Jesus willingly to earth to be that sacrifice. Not only did Jesus die for those who love Him, He died for the ones who hate Him so they, if they choose, would believe the truth, be born again, and have eternal life with Him. He went to the cross for all: rich and poor, young and old, white and black, witches and warlocks. The blood He shed on the cross covers the sin of the world. All who choose to believe in Him will have their sins washed away. God, in His infinite love and mercy, sent His one and only Son into the world to be crucified for the atonement of our sins (Isaiah 53). Jesus was tempted in every way, but lived a perfect life without sin. He was nailed to a cross and was buried. On the third day, He rose from the grave. Hallelujah! His death, burial, and resurrection tore the veil that separated humans from God. Anyone who believes in Him will not perish but have everlasting life through Him. For whomever chooses to believe in Jesus, the spiritual veil that separated him or her from God is removed. God has given us the opportunity to be free from sin and death.

> For this is how God loved the world: He gave His one and only Son, so that everyone who believes in Him will not perish but have eternal life. God sent His Son into the world not to judge the world, but to save the world through Him. (John 3:16–17 NLT)

THE GARDEN

In the Garden of Eden, God provided everything for Adam and Eve. They had food from every seed-bearing plant and from all the fruit trees. God gave them the order and power to rule over all the earth. They reigned over the fish in the sea, the birds in the sky, and all the animals that scurried along the ground. The animals did not prey upon each other for food as they were given every green plant to eat. There was no death. It was perfect, but Eve desired more than what God had provided. She wanted to gain the knowledge of God. One day Satan, who was in the garden in the form of a serpent, asked Eve if God truly said that she and Adam must not eat fruit from any of the trees in the garden. She said they could eat the fruit of every tree except the tree in the middle of the garden, which they were not allowed to eat from or even touch or they would surely die (Genesis 3:2–3). It was the tree of the knowledge of good and evil.

Now the command of the Lord was to not eat the fruit; however, Eve added something extra. She said not only were they not to eat of the fruit, they were not to touch it. In her own understanding, she felt touching the tree was also not allowed. Because she added her own belief about the tree to what God had said, she multiplied her sin.

> But if you have doubts about whether or not you should eat something, you are sinning if you go ahead and do it. For you are not following your convictions. If you do anything you believe is not right, you are sinning. (Romans 14:23 NLT)

Satan responded to Eve and said, "You won't die! God knows that your eyes will be opened as soon as you eat it, and you will be like Him knowing both good and evil" (Genesis 3:4–5 NLT). Temptation was before her eyes. She and Adam had a commandment to follow, but the forbidden fruit of this tree looked so good. Maybe Eve thought to herself, *If I can take one quick bite, it won't be so bad and, in an instant, I can be like God, knowing good and evil*, except neither she nor Adam would be. What happened is what God said would happen if they ate the fruit of that tree: "You shall surely die" (Genesis 2:17 NKJV).

From the very moment Adam and Eve ate of that fruit, death, sickness, and all kinds of evil entered the world. Adam and Eve's temptation led them to rebel against God, opening the door to rebellion for the generations that followed. Eve ate the fruit, then gave some to Adam. This very same scenario has been happening ever since this moment in Eden. God instructs us to do or not do something because of the devastating effects it will have on us, and we do it anyway, seeking to satisfy our own desires, acting on what *we* think is best or based on what makes sense to us.

> For God made Adam first and afterward He made Eve. And it was not Adam who was deceived by Satan. The woman was deceived, and sin was the result. (1 Timothy 2:13–14 NLT)

> Trust in the Lord with all your heart; do not depend on your own understanding. Seek His will in all you do, and He will show you which path to take. (Proverbs 3:5–6 NLT)

THE KINGDOM OF GOD

> For the kingdom of God is not eating and drinking, but righteousness and peace and joy in the Holy Spirit. (Romans 14:17 NKJV)

The kingdom of God is a spiritual kingdom, and it exists inside every person who believes and receives Jesus Christ as his or her Lord and Savior. You can only be made righteous when you believe in Jesus. The moment salvation occurs, the Holy Spirit lives inside of you and His fruit is the manifestation of the kingdom of God within you. This righteousness produces fruit and is a tree of life within you.

> The fruit of the Spirit is love, joy, peace, patience, kindness, goodness, faithfulness, gentleness, and self-control. (Galatians 5:22–23 ESV)

> The fruit of the righteous is a tree of life. (Proverbs 11:30 NKJV)

The very root of this spiritual fruit is love—not love as the world gives but the sacrificial, unconditional love of our Father in heaven and of Jesus. God's banner over us is love and it endures for all time. When you understand and receive this love, you live in the joy of God, the peace of God, the patience of God, the kindness of God, the goodness of God, the faithfulness of God, the gentleness of God, and the self-control of God.

> "For indeed, the kingdom of God is within you." (Luke 17:21 NKJV)

> For the kingdom of God is not in word but in power. (1 Corinthians 4:20 NKJV)

> "But you shall receive power when the Holy Spirit has come upon you." (Acts 1:8 NKJV)

We were created to spend eternity with God. We were created to have a relationship with Him. Many, including me, have asked God, "What is the purpose of my life?" Each person seeks to discover if there is something more to life than the mundane routines carried out daily. Yes, there is something more. God has given us a desire to live forever. In Ecclesiastes 3:11 (NLT), it says, "He planted eternity in the human heart." God planted that seed. When it is watered by His word through teaching, studying, testimony, and prayer, the result is an eternal reward for those who are truly seeking.

> God blesses those who patiently endure testing and temptation. Afterward they will receive the crown of life that God has promised to those who love him. (James 1:12 NLT)

Still, we cannot see the Kingdom of God unless we are born again. When your mother gave birth to you, that was your first birth, a physical birth. We are born into a world of sin, darkness, and death. To enter God's Kingdom, we must be born of the Spirit. This is the second birth, or being born again. In John 3, Jesus explains we must be born of the Spirit to not only see the kingdom but to enter it: "Jesus answered and said to him, 'Most assuredly, I say to you, unless one is born again, he cannot *see* the Kingdom of God'" (John 3:3 NKJV; emphasis added). Then Jesus continued to explain, "Most assuredly, I say to you, unless one is born of water and the Spirit, he cannot *enter* the Kingdom of God (John 3:5 NKJV; emphasis added). It is through Jesus that we receive our new life, one that is everlasting, making us children of God and our bodies temples of the Holy Spirit.

> The Spirit Himself bears witness with our spirit that we are children of God. (Romans 8:16 NKJV)

> Don't you realize that your body is the temple of the Holy Spirit, who lives in you and was given to you by God? You do not belong to yourself. (1 Corinthians 6:19 NLT)

Just as the Kingdom of God produces the fruit of the Spirit, likewise, Satan's kingdom produces rotten fruit. These include being prideful, lying, shedding innocent blood, devising wicked plans, running swiftly towards evil, bearing false witness, sowing discord among people, and being drunk, gluttonous, envious, and idolatrous (Proverbs 6:16–19, 23:21, and14:30).

> Now the works of the flesh are evident, which are: adultery, fornication, uncleanness, lewdness, idolatry, sorcery, hatred, contentions, jealousies, outbursts of wrath, selfish ambitions, dissensions,

heresies, envy, murders, drunkenness, revelries, and the like; of which I tell you beforehand, just as I also told you in time past, that those who practice such things will not inherit the kingdom of God. (Galatians 5:19–21 NKJV)

Chapter 3
LUCIFER

> How you are fallen from heaven, O Lucifer, son of the morning! How you are cut down to the ground, You who weakened the nations! (Isaiah 14:12 NKJV)

Lucifer. The anointed cherub, perfected in beauty from the day he was created until wickedness was found in his heart. He believed he, himself, should be God. He was envious of God's throne. He wanted what God had. He wanted to be worshiped. Lucifer said in his heart, "'I will ascend to heaven and set my throne above God's stars. I will preside on the mountain of the gods far away in the north. I will climb to the highest heavens and be like the Most High'" (Isaiah 14:13–14 NKJV).

By outward appearance, Lucifer was the model of perfection. There was no flaw in his appearance. There was no other heavenly host more beautiful. He was covered in precious stones, and he was full of wisdom. Besides his breathtaking beauty, he was created with tambourines and pipes within him. He was not like any other angel. He was, in fact, an anointed cherub who had access to the Holy Mountain of God and walked among the fiery stones. Lucifer was loved by God. He created him with such perfection, then pride, envy, and covetousness crept into his heart because of his vanity (Ezekiel 28:12–18). His rebellion caused him and a third of the angels who followed him to be banished from heaven, with little access remaining.

> Now there was a day when the sons of God came to present themselves before the Lord, and Satan also came among them. And the Lord said to Satan, "From where do you come?" So Satan answered the Lord and said, "From going to and fro on the earth, and from walking back and forth on it. (Job 1:6–7 NKJV)

> This great dragon—the ancient serpent called the devil, or Satan, the one deceiving the whole world—was thrown down to the earth with all his angels. (Revelation 12:9 NLT)

Once Lucifer was cast down, he became known as the following (all verses are NKJV unless otherwise noted).

- → Serpent—Genesis 3:1
  - ◆ Now the serpent was more cunning than any beast of the field which the Lord God had made.
- → Satan—1 Chronicles 21:1
  - ◆ Now Satan stood up against Israel, and moved David to number Israel.
- → Accuser—Job 1:6
  - ◆ One day the members of the heavenly court came to present themselves before the Lord, and the Accuser, Satan, came with them. (NLT)
- → Devil—Matthew 4:1
  - ◆ Then Jesus was led up by the Spirit into the wilderness to be tempted by the devil.

- → Beelzebub, Ruler of Demons—Matthew 12:24
  - ◆ Now when the Pharisees heard it they said, "This fellow does not cast out demons except by Beelzebub, the ruler of the demons."
- → The Tempter—Mark 1:13
  - ◆ And He was there in the wilderness forty days, tempted by Satan, and was with the wild beasts; and the angels ministered to Him.
- → The Father of Lies—John 8:44
  - ◆ You are of your father the devil, and the desires of your father you want to do. He was a murderer from the beginning, and does not stand in the truth, because there is no truth in him. When he speaks a lie, he speaks from his own resources, for he is a liar and the father of it.
- → Belial—2 Corinthians 6:15
  - ◆ And what accord has Christ with Belial? Or what part has a believer with an unbeliever?
- → Prince of the power of the air—Ephesians 2:1-2
  - ◆ And you He made alive, who were dead in trespasses and sins, in which you once walked according to the course of this world, according to the prince of the power of the air, the spirit who now works in the sons of disobedience
- → Adversary—1 Peter 5:8
  - ◆ Be sober, be vigilant; because your adversary the devil walks about like a roaring lion, seeking whom he may devour.
- → Dragon—Revelation 12:9
  - ◆ So the great dragon was cast out, that serpent of old, called the Devil and Satan, who deceives the whole world; he was cast to the earth, and his angels were cast out with him.

Satan's very nature is rebellious. His goal is to make us like him: rebellious and turned from God. He accomplishes this in many ways, but all of them are meant to occupy our thoughts, setting our minds on anything other than having our eyes set upon God. When we worry, we are meditating on our problem. When we are hurt, we think about that situation and the person who hurt us. When we are angry, we think about how we were wronged. If you are critical of yourself, or base your identity on what your spouse, family members, or friends think about you, this can be your primary focus. If we are offended, feel rejected, or have unforgiveness, especially over a long period of time, a root of bitterness sets in. A root of bitterness is created from replaying over and over in your mind a situation that deeply hurt you, in which you have unforgiveness. This can be difficult to heal—not impossible but difficult.

When the root of a tree becomes diseased, you cannot see it but you know there is something wrong because of the way the rest of the tree looks. The tree may not produce as many leaves. The bark of the tree might appear to be unhealthy. If it is a fruit tree, the fruit might show signs of disease or taste funny. The same goes for a person who has a bitter root. The person's fruit might seem okay from a distance, but on closer inspection is not good. The person can be passive-aggressive, critical, angry, manipulative, and judgmental.

> Look after each other so that none of you fails to receive the grace of God. Watch out that no poisonous root of bitterness grows up to trouble you, corrupting many. (Hebrews 12:15 NLT)

Bitterness causes a person to be stuck in a negative mindset towards others and themselves. Again, this inhibits meditating on Jesus, scripture, and God's plan for your life.

> Then I realized that my heart was bitter, and I was all torn up inside. (Psalm 73:21 NLT)

> Set your mind on things above, not on things on the earth. (Colossians 3:2 NKJV)

Other things that occupy our minds may not even seem harmful but still distract us from God or lead to other problems. All forms of entertainment are prime examples. This includes sports, movies, concerts, bars, clubs, video games, shopping, Netflix, Amazon Prime, and cell phones, just to name a few. It is not only the time that is spent engaged in these activities, but also what is being fed to you through your eyes. Most of the entertainment today is sexualized, feeding the carnal person.

> There is a way that seems right to a man, but its end is the way of death. (Proverbs 14:12 and 16:25 NKJV)

How can Netflix, shopping, video games, or any other entertainment lead to death? For the unbeliever, it is a distraction from Jesus. The worldly hate Christ and seek the riches and pleasures this world has to offer. This path leads to death because the unbelievers choose the world and reject Jesus. For believers, the world's entertainment and pleasures draw them into the world instead of draw them to Jesus and heavenly things. Sometimes, worldly activity can become an idol. Anything in our lives that we desire more than God is idol worship, and the thing is considered a god.

> "You shall have no other gods before Me." (Exodus 20:3 NKJV)

If you are already a follower of Jesus, ask yourself, "Do I desire this thing (whatever it might be) more than I desire Jesus?" Would you be willing to give up your weekly or nightly television show for an opportunity to grow closer to Him? How much are you willing to give up for the One who gave everything up for you? If you give Him your heart and time, it will be the greatest relationship of your life.

Chapter 4
SATAN

I have always been a fan of magic. Every time David Copperfield was on television, there I was, sitting about three feet from my parent's floor model television. I loved it! My favorite part of magic was the illusionists. Their tricks appeared very real. I sat close to the television with the hope of seeing the sleight of hand that would reveal the secret to the trick. No matter how hard I tried, I never saw it.

Merriam-Webster defines an *illusion* as "the state or fact of being intellectually deceived or misled; perception of something objectively existing in such a way as to cause misinterpretation of its actual nature."[1] Satan is the greatest illusionist in the world. The name *devil* is a perfect description of his character. One of the Hebrew meanings of *devil* is "transducer." The *Merriam-Webster* definition of *transducer* is "a device that changes power from one system into another form for another system."[2] Satan takes the things of God and changes them, transforms them, and perverts them for his use in this world, with the sole intention of keeping our eyes off God. He intellectually deceives, misleads,

---

[1] *Merriam-Webster.com Dictionary*, s.v. "illusion," accessed April 22, 2022, https://www.merriam-webster.com/dictionary/illusion.

[2] *Merriam-Webster.com Dictionary*, s.v. "transducer," accessed April 22, 2022, https://www.merriam-webster.com/dictionary/transducer.

misrepresents, and causes our perception of a thing to be distorted. He even created his own satanic trinity.

The Holy Trinity is God the Father, God the Son, and God the Holy Spirit, three in One. The demonic trinity is the Satan, a.k.a. the dragon (who wants to be God), the antichrist, a.k.a. the beast, and the false prophet. They are not three in one.

> And I saw three unclean spirits like frogs coming out of the mouth of the dragon, out of the mouth of the beast, and out of the mouth of the false prophet. (Revelation 16:13 NKJV)

Collectively, every believer in the world makes up the body of Christ and is His Church. Satan also has a church made up of those who oppose Jesus. Besides those who openly declare they worship Satan, most unbelievers don't realize they are a part of his church. They are walking in the dark. Anyone who is not against Jesus is for Him.

> "I know your works, tribulation, and poverty (but you are rich); and I know the blasphemy of those who say they are Jews and are not but are a synagogue [congregation] of Satan." (Revelation 2:9 NKJV)

> For He has rescued us from the kingdom of darkness and transferred us into the Kingdom of His dear Son. (Colossians 1:13 NLT)

God instructs us not to be involved in drunkenness, sexual promiscuity, or immoral living, but in the world we live in today, all these things are the norm because Satan, the god of this world, is the lord of evil. He has deceived those who currently refuse to believe in salvation through Jesus, and convinced them that what they see or believe is correct. This deception keeps them from seeing the truth, the Gospel of Jesus Christ. Satan's path leads to spiritual death. He is a liar and there is no truth found in him (John 8:44).

God passionately desires us to choose His way. He plainly states the two paths we must choose from.

> "Today I have given you the choice between life and death, between blessings and curses. Now I call on heaven and earth to witness the choice you make. *Oh, that you would choose life*, so that you and your descendants might live! (Deuteronomy 30:19 NKJV; emphasis added)

He is literally telling us the answer! Choose life! God gives us the freedom to choose, and He desires for everyone to have eternal life with Him. Choosing life means choosing Jesus. Not choosing Jesus is death. There is only one way to have eternal life and it is through Jesus Christ, our Messiah.

> Jesus said to him, "I am the way, the truth, and the life. No one comes to the Father except through Me." (John 14:6 NKJV)

THE DECEPTION

There are some who believe the devil is real and currently active upon the earth. Others believe he only existed back in the Garden of Eden and no longer affects us. He is, in fact, real. He is highly active in leading thousands astray. How does he deceive so many? In Hosea 4:6 (NKJV), God says, "My people are destroyed for lack of knowledge." In 2 Corinthians 11:14 (NKJV), it says, "And no wonder! For Satan himself transforms himself into an angel of light." Satan deceives because there is a lack of understanding of his ways, of God's way, and, for some, unbelief in both. Satan can blind the minds of unbelievers, but he can't keep anyone from choosing to believe because we all have free will.

Despite the number of years that spanned between Satan deceiving Eve and his attempt to do the same with Jesus in the desert, his method never changed. He used the same three strategies with both Eve and Jesus and uses the same methods today.

The Lust of the Eyes
Eve saw that the tree was beautiful.
Jesus was tempted to turn the stones into loaves of bread.

The Lust of the Flesh
Eve noticed the fruit looked delicious.
Jesus was offered all the kingdoms of the world and their glory.

The Pride of Life
Eve wanted the wisdom she thought the fruit would give her.
Jesus was tempted to prove He was the Son of God by jumping off the top of the temple.

Eve was tempted, just as many of us have been. She saw something that was pleasing to her eyes and began to meditate on it. Satan told her if she ate it, she would be like God, knowing good and evil. This is the same deception that he uses today in attempting to get us to believe what he says instead of what God says. Eve believed Satan, she ate the fruit, and Adam followed suit.

> Now the serpent was more cunning than any beast of the field which the Lord God had made. And he said to the woman, "Has God indeed said, 'You shall not eat of every tree of the garden'?" And the woman said to the serpent, "We may eat the fruit of the trees of the garden; but of the fruit of the tree which is in the midst of the garden, God has said, 'You shall not eat it, nor shall you touch it, lest you die.'" Then the serpent said to the woman, "You will not surely die. For God knows that in the day you eat of it your eyes will be opened, and you will be like God, knowing good and evil." So when the woman saw that the tree was good for food, that it was pleasant to the eyes, and a tree desirable to make one wise, she took of its fruit and ate. She also gave to her husband with her, and he ate. Then the eyes of both of them were opened, and they knew that they were naked; and they sewed fig leaves together and made themselves coverings. (Genesis 3:1–7 NKJV)

One question and two statements from Satan were enough to make Eve stumble. The question was, "'Has God indeed said, "You shall not eat of every tree of the garden?"'"(Genesis 3:1 NKJV). This question planted a demonic seed in her mind. She replied. He kept pushing. He had not achieved his goal, which was to cause her and Adam to rebel against God like he had done. He wanted to steal their perfect home—paradise—bring death, and destroy what God had created for them. Just as Satan was cast out of his perfect dwelling place, and separated from God, he wanted the same outcome for them.

> "You will not surely die. For God knows that in the day you eat of it your eyes will be opened and you will be like God, knowing good and evil." (Genesis 3:4–5 NKJV)

Satan's response said to Adam and Eve that:

→ God is a liar.
→ He (Satan) is telling them the truth.
→ Eating the fruit was no big deal. It would only bring good things to them.
→ God is keeping something from them.
→ He implies that they are blind by telling them their eyes will be opened.
→ He makes them think they will be equal to God.

> For all that is in the world—the lust of the flesh, the lust of the eyes, and the pride of life—is not of the Father but is of the world. (1 John 2:16 NKJV)

SATAN'S WEAPONS

> Stay alert! Watch out for your great enemy, the devil. He prowls around like a roaring lion, looking for someone to devour. (1 Peter 5:8 NLT)

When I first read this verse, and many times after, I imagined Satan using people to attack me or my family. I was looking for an outward sign, one I could physically see. Though he does influence people to do evil works, his number one weapon against all people is psychological.

PSYCHOLOGICAL WARFARE

"Psychological warfare involves the planned use of propaganda and other psychological operations to influence the opinions, emotions, attitudes, and behavior of opposition groups."[3] Just as he did in the garden with Adam and Eve, Satan works to get us to doubt the Word of God. He leads many down false spiritual paths. He wants us to be confused, to worry, to be afraid, to be anxious, and to look to our own strength and resources to resolve any problems. Although we live and experience a physical world, this is not where our battle is. In 2 Corinthians 10:4–5 (NKJV), it says, "For the weapons of our warfare are not carnal but mighty in God for pulling down strongholds, casting down arguments and every high thing that exalts itself against the knowledge of God, bringing every thought into captivity to the obedience of Christ." This verse emphasizes *every* thought, not some thoughts. A stronghold is something a person finds more security, safety, and comfort in than God. It is a dominating mindset or activity. However, God is to be our stronghold.

> The Lord is good, A stronghold in the day of trouble; And He knows those who trust in Him. (Nahum 1:7 NKJV)

Arguments, as mentioned in 2 Corinthians 10:4–5 above, are thoughts that are hostile towards God. In the King James Version, the word *imagination* is used instead of arguments. This pertains to every thought, reason, rationale, idea, philosophy, and theology that opposes God. When these types of thoughts or strongholds are evident, we are instructed to do two things: pull down and

[3] RAND Corporation, "Psychological Warfare," accessed April 2, 2019, https://www.rand.org/topics/psychological-warfare.html.

cast. Pull down those rebellious thoughts and cast them far away. All it takes is one demonic seed to take root for trouble to sprout.

> Satan rose up against Israel and caused David to take a census of the people of Israel. (1 Chronicles 21:1–2 NLT)

> A troublemaker plants seeds of strife. (Proverbs 16:28 NLT)

As believers, we must filter every thought that comes to our minds. We should run them through the filter of the Holy Spirit, so they can be compared to the Word of God. How would you know if a thought is from Satan? First, you must know the Word of God, which means you must read your Bible daily. Our thoughts are transformed when we have the knowledge and wisdom of God to focus on, when we think on things above and not here on the earth. When our spiritual bodies are fed, our souls, minds, wills, and emotions begin to respond.

> For those who live according to the flesh set their minds on the things of the flesh, but those who live according to the Spirit, the things of the Spirit. For to be carnally minded is death, but to be spiritually minded is life and peace. (Romans 8:5–6 NKJV)

While Satan is planting demonic seeds, we must keep busy planting Kingdom seeds. Just as it is God's will that none should perish, as believers it should also be our will.

> It's not important who does the planting, or who does the watering. What's important is that God makes the seed grow. The one who plants and

> the one who waters work together with the same purpose. And both will be rewarded for their own hard work. (1 Corinthians 3:7–9 NLT)

TRICKERY AND DECEIT

Satan will try to get us to believe and follow whatever is false. By pursuing a close relationship with God, you can practice hearing the voice of the Holy Spirit. The Spirit of God leads us into all truth so when He instructs us, it is wise to obey. He would not lead us down a road to destruction, and the Holy Spirit would not try to confuse us. However, Satan will keep trying to bring devastation. He will tempt us in our flesh and our souls. He will also try to use scripture to confuse or trick us into doing something that goes against what God has instructed us to do.

In 1 Kings 13, a prophet was sent to give a message to King Jeroboam, who had done evil things in the sight of the Lord. Fearing he would not be king anymore because the Israelites were returning to Jerusalem to offer sacrifices in the House of the Lord, Jerboam built two golden calves. He told the Israelites those were their gods, and they could offer sacrifices to them. He also created his own feast days, burned incense on his altar, and appointed men to be priests who were not of the priestly line of Levi (1 Kings 12:25–33). When the prophet gave the message to the king, the king became angry, stretched his hand from the altar, and commanded the prophet's arrest. When he did this, his hand withered, and he could not pull it back in. The king asked the prophet to pray for him so that his hand might be restored. The prophet prayed and the king's hand was healed. The king then invited the prophet to come to his house, be refreshed, and get a reward, but the prophet refused because he had instructions from God (1 Kings 13:1–7). The prophet said, "For so it was commanded me by the word of the Lord, saying, 'You shall not eat bread, nor drink water, nor return by the same way you came'" (1 Kings 13:9 NKJV). The prophet did well in obeying what God told him. But Satan does not only try once to get us to stumble. He will keep trying to see if one of his attempts will be successful.

When the prophet was on his way home again, Satan tempted him through an old prophet who tried to get him to go home with him and eat. But he said no. Then the old prophet said, "'I too am a prophet as you are, and an angel spoke to me by the word of the Lord, saying, "Bring him back with you to your house, that he may eat bread and drink water"'" (1 Kings 13:18 NKJV); he was lying to him. Satan's persistence got this prophet to break the command that the Lord gave him. Instead of holding firm to the message God gave him, he believed a false word given to him. He should have asked God if this message was from Him and waited for Him to confirm. Because he assumed what the old prophet said was true, he was disobedient to the word of the Lord, and he was killed by a lion on the road as he continued home (1 Kings 13:11–34). He was deceived.

> Beloved, do not believe every spirit, but test the spirits, whether they are of God; because many false prophets have gone out into the world. (1 John 4:1 NKJV)

It is important for us to renew our minds with God's word every day, so we know exactly what He says and in what context. In Matthew 4:3–10, Satan tried to tempt Jesus by attacking weak points. Since Jesus was on a forty-day fast, the first temptation Satan brought was bread. Then Satan tried to make Jesus fall through pride. Finally, Satan tempted Him with worldly riches. In each circumstance, Jesus used scripture to fight Satan. After the third time, Satan left until another time presented itself for him to attack.

HINDRANCE

Satan will certainly come against you when you take steps in the direction of God. He is threatened by the gifts and callings that God has placed in you. You are a threat to his dark kingdom; therefore, he will attack your peace, try to distract your mind, cause offense, and try to make you doubt hearing God's voice. I have heard these two sayings several times: "If the devil isn't bothering you, you're not moving towards God," and "The higher the level, the bigger the devil." As soon as Jesus was baptized and started His forty-day fast, the devil came to try to get Him to fail.

We can also cause our own spiritual hindrances through unforgiveness, rebellion towards God, false spiritual practices, ungodly soul ties, pride, and lacking desire to know Him more.

Most people struggle with some sort of hindrance in their spiritual walk with God. At times it can be difficult following Christ. Unfortunately, following Jesus does not mean a life of bliss. It can be a difficult journey for us at times, but we have joy because our hope is in Jesus Christ and in our Father in heaven who always watches over us. We have the assurance that He is working things out for us even when we cannot see it.

> We wanted very much to come to you, and I, Paul, tried again and again, but Satan prevented us. (1 Thessalonians 2:18 NLT)

BONDAGE

Spiritual bondage is a form of slavery that keeps us from fully pursuing God. Spiritual bondage occurs from being enslaved to sin. The believer cannot fully live for God, and the non-believer is enslaved to Satan. Some addictions can be hard to overcome. The most recognized forms of enslavement are drugs, alcohol, and pornography. There are certainly other things that can be addictions besides those three. No matter what the addiction is, the chains of that bondage can be broken through Jesus.

> This dear woman, a daughter of Abraham, has been held in bondage by Satan for eighteen years. (Luke 13:16 NLT)

BETRAYAL

Satan inspires betrayal, treason, treachery, infidelity, backstabbing, disloyalty, unfaithfulness, and double crossing. In John 13:2, as the disciples sat down for the Feast of the Passover, the devil had already entered the heart of Judas to cause him to betray Jesus. Satan influenced the heart of Judas through a thought. What is in your mind settles in your heart. What is in your heart will come out through your mouth or through your actions. Every thought that comes into your mind must be examined. If it is not of God, it must be cast away and not allowed for meditation.

> And supper being ended, the devil having already put it into the heart of Judas Iscariot, Simon's son, to betray Him. (John 13:2 NKJV)

LIES

A lie is an untrue statement made with intent to deceive, or to create a false or misleading impression. Satan lied to Eve to cause her and Adam to eat the fruit from the tree of the knowledge of good and evil that God had commanded them not to eat. What lies is Satan telling you today? He could be saying things like, "You're not worthy," "God doesn't want you," "You're not smart," or "You don't have scripture memorized, therefore, how can you do anything in the ministry for God?" Whatever insecurities you might have about yourself, Satan will attack that area, hoping you will agree with what he says instead of believing and agreeing with what God says. Satan is a liar and the father of lies.

> He has always hated the truth because there is no truth in him. When he lies, it is consistent with his character; for he is a liar and the father of lies. (John 8:44 NLT)

> Then Peter said, "Ananias, why have you let Satan fill your heart? You lied to the Holy Spirit, and you kept some of the money for yourself." (Acts 5:3 NLT)

ACCUSATION

In another attempt to hinder our progress towards our divine destiny, Satan will constantly remind us of our sins, planting thoughts of how unworthy we are, and that God could never want us. This is a lie. Jesus gave His life for the world, while we were all still sinners. He considers each one of us worthy; otherwise He would not have given His life so we could be saved from this world and have eternal life with Him. Satan goes before God day and night to bring accusations against you. However, God says when we make Jesus our Lord and Savior, He removes our sin as far as the east is from the west.

> For the accuser of our brothers and sisters has been thrown down to earth—the one who accuses them before our God day and night. (Revelation 12:10 NLT)

TEMPTATION

Satan will attempt to cause you to sin by placing before you what your heart desires: whatever will gratify your flesh or make you feel superior to others. He calls all the carnal pleasures of the world freedom, when in fact they can lead to bondage. The only way we are absolutely free is through Jesus. As we pray, we draw closer to God, and the power of His grace will help us in our weakness.

> No temptation has overtaken you except such as is common to man; but God is faithful, who will not allow you to be tempted beyond what you are able, but with the temptation will also make the way of escape, that you may be able to bear it. (1 Corinthians 10:13 NKJV)

> "Why are you sleeping?" he asked them. "Get up and pray, so that you will not give in to temptation." (Luke 22:46 NLT)

DISGUISE

Satan wraps himself in the things which look good to you, hoping you will take the bait, but his road is disastrous. Studying the Bible to understand the ways of God and the nature of God will help to expose his schemes. This also applies to people who claim to be servants of the Lord but are teaching false doctrine or who are secretly practicing sin. By appearance or charitable deeds, they seem godly. By feeding the homeless, you might believe their teachings must be biblical, but the apostle John says in 1 John 4:1 that we must test every spirit to see if it is of God.

> Even Satan disguises himself as an angel of light. So it is no wonder that his servants also disguise themselves as servants of righteousness. (2 Corinthians 11:14–15 NLT)

> This man will come to do the work of Satan with counterfeit power and signs and miracles. He will use every kind of evil deception to fool those on their way to destruction, because they refuse to love and accept the truth that would save them. (2 Thessalonians 2:9–10 NLT)

DISEASE

There are various causes of disease: heredity, genes, infections, poor dietary choices, or lack of exercise, to name a few. Yet there are some diseases, whether mental or physical, that can be caused by a spirit of infirmity. These are spirits that enter a person through sin, trauma, or a curse and cause physical ailments or mental disorders. Some of these spirits attacking the mind can cause thoughts of suicide or deep depression. They can cause pain that cannot be definitively diagnosed. A common open door for this spirit to enter is unforgiveness.

> And behold, there was a woman who had a spirit of infirmity eighteen years, and was bent over and could in no way raise herself up. (Luke 13:11 NKJV)

> Now a certain man was there who had an infirmity thirty-eight years. (John 5:5 NKJV)

> When evening had come, they brought to Him many who were demon-possessed. And He cast out the spirits with a word, and healed all who were sick. (Matthew 8:16 NKJV)

MURDER

Besides the obvious taking of someone's life, the Bible teaches that we can bring death to someone or ourselves by our words.

> Death and life are in the power of the tongue, And those who love it will eat its fruit. (Proverbs 18:21 NKJV)

There is nothing more prevalent in our world today than the message of "I have the right to be heard." Satan would have us believe that our words are not that important, therefore, say what you will. This is a lie. We each have the power to speak spiritual life into someone or bring spiritual death. Jesus came that we would have not only life but life more abundantly. We want to offer and pass this same life that Jesus gave to us onto others. God says we will eat the fruit of what we speak. When we give to others the sweet fruit of the Holy Spirit (love, joy, peace, longsuffering, kindness, goodness, faithfulness, gentleness, self-control), we will be blessed and blessed by God. The words and actions of the enemy (hate, slander, gossip, unloving) only seek to steal, kill, and destroy.

> A man shall eat well by the fruit of his mouth, But the soul of the unfaithful feeds on violence. He who guards his mouth preserves his life, But he who opens wide his lips shall have destruction. (Proverbs 13:2–3 NKJV)

> "For by your words you will be justified, and by your words you will be condemned." (Matthew 12:37 NKJV)

> "If the Son makes you free, you shall be free indeed." (John 8:36 NKJV)

Satan, on the other hand, will not step out of your way so you can have that freedom. We must boldly take what we have rightly inherited through Jesus' death on the cross.

> And from the days of John the Baptist until now the kingdom of heaven suffers violence, and the violent take it by force. (Matthew 11:12 NKJV)

For this reason, we are told to put on our armor (Ephesians 6:14-17). The very first piece we are instructed to put on is the Belt of Truth. In John 8:32 (NKJV), Jesus said, "And you shall know the truth, <u>and the truth shall make you free</u>." The last piece of our armor is the Sword of the Spirit, which is the Word of God. Our spiritual gear starts with the Word and ends with the Word. All other parts of our equipment are listed between. Knowing the word of God is how we get our freedom. We must know scripture (belt) to know who we are in Christ (breastplate), to be able to bring peace (shoes), to have faith in God (shield), to filter out the thoughts of the enemy and meditate on what is true (helmet), and to stand on our authority in Christ and skillfully use the word of God (sword). We are to put on our spiritual armor so we can be properly equipped to fight. Put on:

> Belt of Truth—Know Scripture
> Breastplate of Righteousness —Know your position through Christ
> Shoes of peace—Bring peace/leave peace

Shield of faith—Have faith because God is faithful
Helmet of salvation —Guard your mind
Sword of the Spirit—Know the Word of God

Our armor is held together by prayer. It strengthens us through the Holy Spirit and draws us closer to God so we can stand firm against the devil in any situation.

> Praying always with all prayer and supplication in the Spirit, being watchful to this end with all perseverance and supplication for all the saints. (Ephesians 6:18 NKJV)

When we equip ourselves the way God intended, no situation made to break us will succeed. God causes all things to work together for the good of those who love Him and are called according to His purpose. If you have a desire in your heart to know Jesus, you are called.

> A final word: Be strong in the Lord and in his mighty power. Put on all of God's armor so that you will be able to stand firm against all strategies of the devil. For we are not fighting against flesh-and-blood enemies, but against evil rulers and authorities of the unseen world, against mighty powers in this dark world, and against evil spirits in the heavenly pla.ces. Therefore, put on every piece of God's armor so you will be able to resist the enemy in the time of evil. (Ephesians 6:10–13 NKJV)

Chapter 5

THE PARABLE OF THE SOWER

> "Therefore if the Son makes you free, you shall be free indeed." (John 8:36 NKJV)

"I don't feel free." I used to say these words to myself all the time. I've heard others say them too. How can I be free when I feel anxious, worried, depressed, and burdened by all of life's problems? I spent several years trying to answer this question. I called out to the Lord because I didn't understand. "Lord, how come the money hasn't appeared for this bill? How will my car get fixed? How will I pay for childcare so I can work? It's so expensive. I thought You would take care of me and help me?" It is not God's will that we suffer.

> For God chose to save us through our Lord Jesus Christ, not to pour out his anger on us. (1 Thessalonians 5:9 NLT)

It all came down to one thing. I did not trust God.

"I'll believe it when I see it." I believe this could be the official motto of the world. Again, beginning in the Garden of Eden, Adam and Eve found hope in what they thought they were going to gain from eating the fruit. Satan was able to redirect Adam and Eve's focus from what God had given them (dominion over all the earth, and every fruit tree and herb that yields seed) onto a lie about what they could have by eating it. Instead of believing that God had given them everything good, they believed the lies planted by the devil and ate from the one tree prohibited by God.

At times worry and fear fill our minds because of certain situations. They can cause us to doubt what God has said about who we are and the great inheritance we have with Him. John 8:36, written above, manifests that freedom when we wholeheartedly believe the word of God, trust that He does not lie, be patient in His plans for us, and know that He is not maliciously withholding from us. We experience freedom when we act on our faith.

When your first place of refuge is something secular (worldly), that makes it hard for faith to grow.

> Don't let anyone capture you with empty philosophies and high-sounding nonsense that come from human thinking and from the spiritual powers of this world, rather than from Christ. For in Christ lives all the fullness of God in a human body. So <u>you also are complete through your union with Christ</u>, who is the head over every ruler and authority. (Colossians 2:8–10 NLT)

For our faith to grow, we must hear and act on the Word of God.

> So then faith comes by hearing, and hearing by the word of God. (Romans 10:17 NKJV)

What does it mean to "act on" the Word of God? It means no matter what your situation is, you respond according to what God has said. As Paul and Silas were in prison, they continued to trust in God. They had peace within themselves even though they were in prison. Their reaction to their situation was observed by the other prisoners—a testimony of Jesus Christ. As a result of their faith, others were set free. Your life can also be a testimony of the goodness of God by your decision to praise God no matter your circumstances.

> But at midnight Paul and Silas were praying and singing hymns to God, and the prisoners were listening to them. Suddenly there was a great earthquake, so that the foundations of the prison were shaken; and immediately all the doors were opened and everyone's chains were loosed. (Acts 16:25–26 NKJV)

YOUR ENVIRONMENT

Acting on the Word of God can prove to be difficult when what is being taken into your mind and heart is not a source of life.

> "It is the Spirit who gives life; the flesh profits nothing. The words that I speak to you are spirit, and they are life." (John 6:63 NKJV)

You can almost look in any direction in this world to experience something to make you feel sad or hopeless. It can come from witnessing other people's circumstances or from our own hardships. These non-life giving seeds could come from negative or abusive words spoken by family, friends, co-workers, your spouse, yourself, or from television programs, radio, internet sites, or social media—in other words, your environment.

Sometimes the consequences of our environment are not immediately apparent. To compare, consider secondhand smoke. The Centers for Disease Control and Prevention (CDC) defines secondhand smoke as "the combination of smoke from the burning end of a cigarette and the smoke breathed out by smokers." They have warned the public numerous times about the dangers of secondhand cigarette smoke. For a nonsmoker, it may seem harmless to be in the presence of friends, family, or coworkers who are smoking. Occasionally inhaling the smoke may not be comfortable, but some tolerate it, believing it is not a big deal since it is for a brief period. However, the CDC states, "Secondhand smoke contains more than 7,000 chemicals. Hundreds are toxic and about 70 can cause cancer. Since the 1964 Surgeon General's Report, 2.5 million adults who were nonsmokers died because they breathed secondhand smoke."[4] Two and a half million people have died from toxicities in their environment put there by someone else. Spiritually speaking, you as the nonsmoker (the believer) should not tolerate any toxins in your atmosphere from smokers (non-believers or carnal Christians). We must evaluate our own environment and extinguish what is harmful in what we hear, see, and speak.

> Let the word of Christ dwell in you richly in all wisdom, teaching and admonishing one another in psalms and hymns and spiritual songs, singing with grace in your hearts to the Lord. (Colossians 3:16 NKJV)

---

[4] Centers For Disease Control and Prevention, Health Effects of Secondhand Smoke, last updated January 11, 2017, https://www.cdc.gov/tobacco/data_statistics/fact_sheets/secondhand_smoke/health_effects/index.htm.

WHO YOU ARE

Jesus said in John 10 that His sheep hear His voice and the voice of stranger they will not follow. When we become children of God through Jesus, we gain not only a new residence but a new identity. We must no longer agree with the world's view of who we are. We must receive what Jesus says about us because what He says is truth. Any voice in your life that speaks words contrary to what God says must be cast away.

> My victory and honor come from God alone. He is my refuge, a rock where no enemy can reach me. (Psalm 62:7 NLT)

> For the Lord your God is going with you! He will fight for you against your enemies, and He will give you victory! (Deuteronomy 20:4 NLT)

We belong to a Kingdom which is not of this world and, indeed, we are ambassadors of Christ (John 18:36; 2 Corinthians 5:20).

> If anyone is in Christ, he is a new creation; old things have passed away; behold, all things have become new. (2 Corinthians 5:17 NKJV)

An *ambassador* is "a diplomatic agent of the highest rank accredited to a foreign government or sovereign as the resident representative of his or her own government or sovereign or appointed for a special and often temporary diplomatic assignment."[5] We are high-ranking agents for the Kingdom of God here on earth to carry out God's assignments. Then on the

[5] Merriam-Webster.com Dictionary, s.v. "ambassador," accessed April 2, 2019, https://www.merriam-webster.com/dictionary/ambassador.

appointed day, of which no one knows the day or hour, we will suddenly be with our Lord (Matthew 24:36).

What Is It That God Says about His Children?

Before you were born, He chose you (Galatians 1:15).

You are redeemed (Isaiah 43:1).

You have eternal life through Jesus (Matthew 19:29).

You are loved (Ephesians 1:4).

You are a child of God (Galatians 3:26).

You have been adopted into His family (Ephesians 1: 5).

Through Jesus, you are righteous (Romans 5:17).

You have been made right in His sight (Romans 3:24).

You have the mind of Christ (1 Corinthians 2:16).

He keeps you strong to the end (1 Corinthians 1:8).

You have an incorruptible and undefiled inheritance reserved for you in heaven (1 Peter 1:3–5).

These are only a few of the many things God says and you can be sure that what He says is true because God does not lie.

> God is not a man, so He does not lie. He is not human, so He does not change His mind. (Numbers 23:19 NLT)

THE PARABLE OF THE SOWER

In Matthew 13, Mark 4, and Luke 8 is the Parable of the Sower. This parable describes a man who is sowing seeds. The seeds fall in various places, producing different results. As I read each account of this parable, as told by Matthew, Mark, and Luke, the Lord showed me something. He showed me this parable is talking about the spiritual life of the believer. First, He reveals the places the seed landed are the stages in our journey with the Lord. Not everyone goes through these in this order, but I believe at one time or another, most believers, if not every believer, have experienced these situations. Second, He reveals that as believers (sowers), we have a choice of where we sow our seed.

THE SPIRITUAL JOURNEY

- Footpath
  - The first place listed where some of the seed fell is the footpath. This represents those who hear the word of God but can't receive it because they don't understand. The seed is trampled on by situations in life, and Satan immediately takes it away. It is hard to grab hold of the truth when you are struggling to understand how it applies to your life.
    - In the early days, before I seriously gave my life to Jesus, many people would talk to me about Him, but I never understood. I pondered what was said but ended up living as I wanted, partially

out of the frustration of not understanding. Satan plucked those seeds from me. Living in rebellion against God seemed almost easier than trying to understand how the Bible fit into my life. It was much later that I would see that the Bible does not fit into my life, but my life is in the Bible, in Jesus.

> My people are destroyed for lack of knowledge. (Hosea 4:6 NKJV)
>
> "The devil comes and takes away the word out of their hearts, lest they should believe and be saved." (Luke 8:12 NKJV)
>
> For you died, and your life is hidden with Christ in God. (Colossians 3:3 NKJV)

- Rocky Soil
  - The seed that fell on the stony ground sprouted a plant with shallow roots. When the hot sun was on it, the plant, lacking water, was scorched and died. This is the time when someone receives the Word of God with joy. It could be a temporary word of encouragement, of comfort, of hope. I say temporary because it is a word that satisfies for the moment but imparts no real trust in God. The person believes what He says even when the situation looks grim, yet has no faith. When a problem arises or gets worse or persecution comes, that plant of joy that sprung up will die because no roots grew deeper down into God. It wasn't watered by the Word. When the heat

of life's issues begins to burn, you might last a little while, but soon you stumble.

- I gladly received biblical encouragement from many people in my life but again, I had no understanding. I was not reading my Bible, which I felt intimidated by. I did not understand the ways of God. I had faith as long as God was on my schedule. When God didn't meet my need in the time I thought He should, I took the matter into my own hands, leaning on my own understanding.

> As you therefore have received Christ Jesus the Lord, so walk in Him, rooted, and built up in Him and established in the faith, as you have been taught, abounding in it with thanksgiving. (Colossians 2:6–7 NKJV)

- Among Thorns
  - Some seeds that fell among the thorns. As the seeds sprouted, the thorns came up too and choked the plant so it produced no fruit. In short, this is the carnal Christian. In Luke's account of this parable, those who receive the word in this condition "bring no fruit to maturity" (Luke 8:14 NKJV). As the Word of God is being poured into them, they are also living like the rest of the world. They want the blessings of God but are not ready to let go of worldly desires. The plant that begins to grow from God's Kingdom seeds will be choked out by the thorny plant of the world. For the world to have eternal life through Him, Jesus had to take the punishment for the sin of the world upon

Himself. One of the ways He was brutalized was by the soldiers putting a crown of thorns on His head. Those thorns represent the sin of the world.

- I started going to church regularly and doing Bible studies. I was learning more about Jesus, but again, I was still doing worldly activities, never understanding I was not to blend in with the world but live a life separate from the world.

> Then Pilate had Jesus flogged with a lead-tipped whip. The soldiers wove a crown of thorns and put it on his head, and they put a purple robe on him. (John 19:1–2 NLT)

> Now he who received seed among the thorns is he who hears the word, and the cares of this world and the deceitfulness of riches choke the word, and he becomes unfruitful. (Matthew 13:22 NKJV)

> Adulterers and adulteresses! Do you not know that friendship with the world is enmity with God? Whoever therefore wants to be a friend of the world makes himself an enemy of God. (James 4:4 NKJV)

- Good Soil
  - The seed that fell on this ground produced a crop and increased. This is the believer who, with an honest and good heart, hears the word of God, keeps it, understands it, accepts it, and with perseverance, bears fruit. This is the believer who has discovered the importance of having a relationship with Jesus, with Father God, and with the Holy Spirit. They understand how they must have a heart free from unforgiveness, bitterness, and deception because these things hinder their spiritual walks. As difficulties in life come about, they persevere. We all have troubling situations that pop up in our lives, however, the key is to not let them overtake us but to walk in faith, keeping our eyes on the Lord, trusting and believing that He has a plan and watches over us. Trials are where we grow. If we did not have them, we would stay in the same spiritual place, never maturing, never learning lessons, or becoming closer to God. Trials are where our faith increases. Sometimes the solution to an issue seems impossible and the only way it could work is if God did something. When you see God work in the impossible situation, your faith gets a boost because you have experienced His faithfulness. Nothing is impossible for Him.
    - Making the decision to lay my life down at the feet of Jesus and setting aside at least an hour with Him every day was the greatest thing I could have done. This is when my life began to change.

> But we also glory in tribulations, knowing that tribulation produces perseverance; and perseverance, character; and character, hope.

> Now hope does not disappoint, because the love of God has been poured out in our hearts by the Holy Spirit who was given to us. (Romans 5:3–5 NKJV)

> If they obey and serve Him, they shall spend their days in prosperity, And their years in pleasures. (Job 36:11 NKJV)

THE SOWER

As you draw closer to God, you begin to see things in a different light—His light. What used to entertain you does not entertain you anymore. Things you used to spend money on, you no longer do. You begin to look outside your own needs and look for ways to bless and serve others. Your faith and trust in God increase to a greater level.

Matthew 25:14–30 is the Parable of the Talents. A man traveling to a far country left talents with His servants. He left with each servant an amount according to his ability. With the one man, He left five talents. That servant multiplied what was given to him and gained five more. Another was left two talents. This servant also multiplied what was given to him and he gained two more. In each of these instances, the Master said, "Well done, good and faithful servant" (Matthew 25:21–23 NKJV). The servant who was left with one talent, out of fear did nothing with it, so he gained nothing. Are you working to multiply the talent (ability or craft) the Lord has given you? Where are you sowing your seeds of time, money, and skills?

In Philippians 3:14 (NKJV), the apostle Paul said, "I press toward the goal for the prize of the upward call of God in Christ

Jesus." This upward call is God calling us into His Kingdom. We forget the things of the past and reach forward to those things which are ahead (Philippians 3:13). This is Kingdom thinking. When you think about the things above, you begin to live from above. This is the Kingdom of God. Kingdom thinking leads to Kingdom living. To live according to God and not this world is freedom.

> If then you were raised with Christ, seek those things which are above, where Christ is, sitting at the right hand of God. Set your mind on things above, not on things on the earth. (Colossians 3:1–2 NKJV)

When you begin to sow your seeds on Kingdom ground, you will yield a crop; some thirty, some sixty, some a hundredfold.

> "But he who received seed on the good ground is he who hears the word and understands it, who indeed bears fruit and produces: some a hundredfold, some sixty, some thirty." (Matthew 13:23 NKJV)

> "You did not choose Me, but I chose you and appointed you that you should go and bear fruit, and that your fruit should remain, that whatever you ask the Father in My name He may give you." (John 15:16 NKJV)

Chapter 6
THE DOOR

> "I am the door. If anyone enters by Me, he will be saved, and will go in and out and find pasture." (John 10:9 NKJV)

Many people are familiar with the story of Moses. God spoke to him from a burning bush on the mountain. He revealed to Moses the plan He had for his life. He told Moses that he was going to lead the Israelites out of the bondage of Egyptian slavery. Pharaoh was so hard-hearted, refusing to release them, that God sent many plagues upon the land and people of Egypt. He turned the water to blood, and sent frogs, lice, flies, livestock disease, boils, hail, locusts, and darkness. None of these was enough to make Pharaoh set the Israelites free. The tenth plague was the death of the firstborn; the first born of Pharaoh, the firstborn of the captives who were in prison, and the firstborn of livestock. But the Israelites were protected from the destroyer who passed over the land to bring death. God called Moses and the elders of Israel. He told them to pick lambs according to their families and kill them. These are the Passover lambs. They were then to take the lambs' blood and wipe it across the tops of their doors and on each doorpost.

> "For the Lord will pass through to strike the Egyptians; and when He sees the blood on the lintel and on the two doorposts, the Lord will pass over the door and not allow the destroyer to come into your houses to strike you." (Exodus 12:23 NKJV)

The Lord's Passover is much more detailed than what is listed here, but for this chapter, the focus is the door.

The Passover that God instituted foreshadowed of the death of Christ, who would come and shed His blood for the world. It was a physical act of putting the blood of the lamb over the tops and sides of the doors. In John 10:9 (NKJV), Jesus said, "I am the door." Jesus, our Lamb, was already slain for us. By opening the doors of our hearts to Him, we are spiritually putting His blood over the doorposts of our hearts. Whoever believes in Him, will be covered by His blood, and enter through that spiritual door (Jesus) into eternal life.

Jesus clearly states that He is *the* Door that we must enter to be saved. He is not *a* door, leaving us with the idea that there are other ways to gain eternal life and have our names written in the Book of Life.

> There is no other name under heaven given among men by which we must be saved. (Acts 4:12 NKJV)

A popular lie of the enemy is that there are many ways to get to heaven; however, there is only one: Jesus. Naturally speaking, doors are used to enter and exit, to keep people out, and to shut people in. There is one thing Jesus requires of us before He lets us enter. We must first open the door to Him and ask Him to come inside. When the salvation message is given (this is Jesus knocking), and we say, "Yes" (we are opening the door), Jesus comes in (by the Holy Spirit He lives inside us). Oftentimes, people slam this door in Jesus's face. They are not ready to receive Him or they do not want to believe.

> "'Behold, I stand at the door and knock. If anyone hears My voice and opens the door, I will come in to him and dine with him, and he with Me.'" (Revelation 3:20NKJV)

There are also doors of opportunity. In this world, we must wait for someone else to find us talented enough, worthy enough, or promising enough that we would succeed in a particular position if given the chance. But with God, we do not have to work hard enough or compete with someone else for a position in His house. All He needs is our continued "Yes!" to Him every day, and we get to walk through the door provided for us and begin an unbelievable journey with Him.

> "In My Father's house are many mansions; if it were not so, I would have told you. I go to prepare a place for you." (John 14:2 NKJV)

Once we enter, there is nothing that can separate us from Him, except our own choice to walk away.

> For I am persuaded that neither death nor life, nor angels nor principalities nor powers, nor things present nor things to come, nor height nor depth, nor any other created thing, shall be able to separate us from the love of God which is in Christ Jesus our Lord. (Romans 8:38–39NKJV)

Jesus enters our houses by the doors that we open to Him, as explained above. But there are those who try to enter our houses through other ways.

> "Most assuredly, I say to you, he who does not enter the sheepfold by the door, but climbs up some other way, the same is a thief and a robber. But he who enters by the door is the shepherd of the sheep." (John 10:1-2 NKJV)

Whoever tries to enter by another way is the same as a thief and a robber. A thief secretly sneaks in and takes what is not his or hers. A robber is one who takes what is not his or hers by force or violence. These thieves are the ones who steer people away from the Way to eternal life. They are:

→ Pharisees/Sadducees: Religious leaders who teach that the way to get to heaven is by following the law, by obeying a set of rules and regulations.

> "Woe to you, scribes and Pharisees, hypocrites! For you travel land and sea to win one proselyte, and when he is won, you make him twice as much a son of hell as yourselves." (Matthew 23:15 NKJV)

→ Thieves: Satan; as in the Parable of the Sower, plucks away scriptural seeds that have been sown in you to cause confusion and lack of understanding of the word. Guard the word that has been sown into you.

> "But know this, that if the master of the house had known what hour the thief would come, he would have watched and

> not allowed his house to be broken into." (Matthew 24:43 NKJV)

- → False Teachers: Those who preach something other than Jesus.

> But there were also false prophets among the people, even as there will be false teachers among you, who will secretly bring in destructive heresies, even denying the Lord who bought them, and bring on themselves swift destruction. And many will follow their destructive ways, because of whom the way of truth will be blasphemed. (2 Peter 2:1–2 NKJV)

- → Robbers: They use physical force to take what they please.

> "If thieves had come to you, If robbers by night—Oh, how you will be cut off!—Would they not have stolen till they had enough?" (Obadiah 1:5 NKJV)

Satan is busy at work, watching, waiting, and looking for an opportunity to lead us astray. He uses false teachings, deception, temptation, and other ways to try to knock us off the narrow path of God. He seeks openings in our houses (souls, minds, wills, emotions) that he can enter and dwell. Sometimes we are not aware that we've made a way for him to enter. However, just as we secure the doors and windows in our physical houses, we must do the same for our spiritual houses.

> You shall keep the watch of the house, lest it be broken down. (2 Kings 11:6 NKJV)

Chapter 7

KEEP WATCH OVER YOUR HOUSE

> "No one can enter a strong man's house and plunder his goods, unless he first binds the strong man. And then he will plunder his house." (Mark 3:27 NKJV)

It has always been the desire of God to dwell with His children.

> And they heard the sound of the Lord God walking in the garden in the cool of the day. (Genesis 3:8 NKJV)

Even after Adam and Eve ate the forbidden fruit, causing a separation between God and humans, God still desired to be with us.

> "Behold, I am with you and will keep you wherever you go." (Genesis 28:15 NKJV)

> "Be strong and of good courage, do not fear nor be afraid of them; for the Lord your God, He is

> the One who goes with you. He will not leave you nor forsake you." (Deuteronomy 31:6 NKJV)

As amazing as it was that God was with the Israelites, He had an even greater plan, which has indeed been fulfilled. No longer was God going to be with His children in a cloud or pillar of fire, but His Spirit, the Holy Spirit, would live inside everyone who has been born again. Our bodies have been transformed by the new birth into the dwelling places of the Holy Spirit.

> Jesus answered and said to him, "If anyone loves Me, he will keep My word; and My Father will love him, and We will come to him and make Our home with him. (John 14:23 NKJV)

> Do you not know that you are the temple of God and that the Spirit of God dwells in you? (1 Corinthians 3:16 NKJV)

Exactly where does the Holy Spirit reside within us? In 1 Thessalonians 5:23 (NKJV), the apostle Paul says, "Now may the God of peace Himself sanctify you completely; and may your whole spirit, soul, and body be preserved blameless at the coming of our Lord Jesus Christ." We are three parts: spirit, soul, and body. Notice the order that the apostle Paul gives. He lists spirit first. This is significant because we are to live by the Spirit first.

> For you were once darkness, but now you are light in the Lord. Walk as children of light (for the fruit of the Spirit is in all goodness, righteousness, and truth), finding out what is acceptable to the Lord. (Ephesians 5:8–10 NKJV)

The Holy Spirit lives in the spirit part of our temple. When we are born again, our spirit, not our souls, are made new. Before getting saved, we lived from our souls, but once we are born again, we must live by the Spirit.

> I will give you a new heart and put a new spirit within you; I will take the heart of stone out of your flesh and give you a heart of flesh. I will put My Spirit within you and cause you to walk in My statutes, and you will keep My judgments and do them. (Ezekiel 36:26–27 NKJV)

To experience this new life, our minds, wills, and emotions must be brought under the submission of our spirits.

> For those who live according to the flesh set their minds on the things of the flesh, but those who live according to the Spirit, the things of the Spirit. For to be carnally minded is death, but to be spiritually minded is life and peace. Because the carnal mind is enmity against God; for it is not subject to the law of God, nor indeed can be. (Romans 8:5–7 NKJV)

Naturally, we want to satisfy our flesh. We want what feels good, or to say what we please. We want things our way, but that is selfish. In our temples (our bodies), we have been given a beautiful room (new spirit) with a gorgeous view (through the eyes of God). We must learn to live from this room instead of the rooms in our soul which are unstable and change daily. This new living arrangement (living from the spirit) will manifest a transformed life when we begin to live by God's will and not our own.

> And do not be conformed to this world, but be transformed by the renewing of your mind, that you may prove what is that good and acceptable and perfect will of God. (Romans 12:2 NKVJ)

> The instructions of the Lord are perfect, reviving the soul. The decrees of the Lord are trustworthy, making wise the simple. (Psalms 19:7 NLT)

LEGAL RIGHTS

A legal right is an act which gives demons access in your life. They are given this right through either personal sin, sins of others against you, or the sins of ancestors. The practice of sinning opens the door to the enemy. In John 8:44 (NKJV), Jesus told the Pharisees, "You are of your father the devil, and the desires of your father you want to do. He was a murderer from the beginning, and does not stand in the truth, because there is no truth in him. When he speaks a lie, he speaks from his own resources, for he is a liar and the father of it." He states that the Pharisees are of their father, the devil, because the desires of their hearts are the same as the devil's. Anything we do that is a part of the kingdom of darkness, against God, is the legal right, the access, which Satan uses to attack us. There are several verses that list the possible access (all NKJV):

> These six things the Lord hates, Yes, seven are an abomination to Him: A proud look, a lying tongue, hands that shed innocent blood, a heart that devises wicked plans, feet that are swift in running to evil, a false witness who speaks lies, and one who sows discord among brethren. (Proverbs 6:16–19)

For rebellion is as the sin of witchcraft, and stubbornness is as iniquity and idolatry. (1 Samuel 15:23)

Don't you realize that those who do wrong will not inherit the Kingdom of God? Don't fool yourselves. Those who indulge in sexual sin, or who worship idols, or commit adultery, or are male prostitutes, or practice homosexuality, or are thieves, or greedy people, or drunkards, or are abusive, or cheat people—none of these will inherit the Kingdom of God. (1 Corinthians 6:9–10)

"Do not turn to idols, nor make for yourselves molded gods: I am the Lord your God." (Leviticus 19:4)

"You shall not hate your brother in your heart." (Leviticus 19:17)

Let all bitterness, wrath, anger, clamor, and evil speaking be put away from you, with all malice. (Ephesians 4:31)

When you follow the desires of your sinful nature, the results are very clear: sexual immorality, impurity, lustful pleasures, idolatry, sorcery, hostility, quarreling, jealousy, outbursts of anger, selfish ambition, dissension, division, envy, drunkenness, wild parties, and other sins like these. Let me tell you again, as I have before, that anyone living that sort of life will not inherit the Kingdom of God. (Galatians 5:19–21)

Satan seeks to get you out of the will of God through sin/rebellion with the end goal of sending people to hell. For as long as we are on this earth, he will keep trying. This means we must do our part. Following Jesus is not a passive faith. We are the hands, feet, mouth, and heart of God. We can be effective in our spiritual walks by His Holy Spirit who lives in us.

As Satan is busy planting seeds, we too must be busy planting Kingdom seeds for God, and this includes planting seeds inside ourselves, watering them with the Word of God. We must walk in the Spirit. To walk by the Spirit, we cannot think in the flesh. This means we cannot expect the blessings that God has if we are living a life that looks like the rest of the world that is unsaved.

> If we live in the Spirit, let us also walk in the Spirit. (Galatians 5:25 NKJV)

OPEN DOORS

> You shall keep the watch of the house, lest it be broken down. (2 Kings 11:6 NKJV)

We have spiritual doors. They are our eyes, ears, and mouths. It is through these areas that either heavenly seeds or demonic seeds are planted. If a seed is sown by the enemy and it is meditated on, next will come the action—the open door. Sin is the open door which creates the legal right for demons to usher their way in. Eve meditated on the seed of the enemy. She listened to the lie from the devil, she spoke to him and misquoted God, she gazed at the fruit, she thought about it, then acted on her thought. Sometimes demons enter a person by a legal right for something that was not his or her fault. Examples include child abuse, trauma, molestation, a family history of idolatry, witchcraft, rituals, vows, oaths, or generational curses. Regardless of the situation, demons have limited rights to torment a person because Jesus stripped them of their power through His death on the cross. Whether you belong to God or not, demons can enter you and live in your soul.

→ Job was a man of God yet was tormented by Satan.
Then the Lord said to Satan, "Have you considered My servant Job, that there is none like him on the earth, a blameless and upright man, one who fears God and shuns evil?" (Job 1:8 NKJV)

→ Judas Iscariot was chosen by Jesus, was one of the twelve disciples, and Satan entered him.
Then Satan entered Judas, surnamed Iscariot, who was numbered among the twelve. (Luke 22:3 NKJV)

→ Ananias and Sapphira were believers when Satan entered them.
But a certain man named Ananias, with Sapphira his wife, sold a possession. And he kept back part of the proceeds, his wife also being aware of it, and brought a certain part and laid it at the apostles' feet. But Peter said, "Ananias, why has Satan filled your heart to lie to the Holy Spirit and keep back part of the price of the land for yourself?" (Acts 5:1–3 NKJV)

Satan desires to trap us. He watches and waits for his opportunity.

"If you do well, will you not be accepted? And if you do not do well, sin lies at the door. And its desire is for you, but you should rule over it." (Genesis 4:7 NKJV)

> "Take heed to yourselves, lest your heart be deceived, and you turn aside and serve other gods and worship them." (Deuteronomy 11:16 NKJV)

This is not to say that there is a demon behind every bush, however, there is a demon behind every bush. There is a real spiritual battle for your soul. The enemy never stops trying to misguide people. By reading the Bible, praying, and spending time with God, you will be able to discern between the voice of the enemy and the Holy Spirit. Despite Satan's attacks, our God is bigger. He never sleeps but watches over us always. He is working on our behalf, even while we sleep.

> The eyes of the Lord are in every place, keeping watch on the evil and the good. (Proverbs 15:3 NKJV)

> The Lord himself watches over you! The Lord stands beside you as your protective shade. (Psalm 121:5 NKJV)

> I lay down and slept, yet I woke up in safety, for the Lord was watching over me. (Psalm 3:5 NKJV)

Our war is not against what we can see but against what we cannot see.

> For we do not wrestle against flesh and blood, but against principalities, against powers, against the rulers of the darkness of this age, against spiritual hosts of wickedness in the heavenly places. (Ephesians 6:12 NKJV)

EYE GATE

> I will set nothing wicked before my eyes. (Psalms 101:3 NKJV)

> I made a covenant with my eyes not to look with lust at a young woman [man]. (Job 31:1 NLT)

Lust defined is an intense longing. This word is usually associated with a sexual reference; however, it can also be an intense longing for money, drugs, alcohol, material things, or food. Eve looked lustfully upon the fruit of the forbidden tree, the tree of the knowledge of good and evil. She had an intense longing for the fruit and a distorted view of what having it might do for her.

In Job 31:7–8 (NLT), Job states that lust in the heart can enter through the eye. He said, "If I have strayed from his pathway, or if my heart has lusted for what my eyes have seen, or if I am guilty of any other sin, then let someone else eat the crops I have planted. Let all that I have planted be uprooted." Then he said, "For lust is a shameful sin, a crime that should be punished. It is a fire that burns all the way to hell. It would wipe out everything I own" (Job 31:11–12 NLT). Lust can become a wildfire, burning out of control and destroying not only those people's lives, but the lives of those around them. Wildfires begin when the environment is right for a fire to rapidly spread when a spark of some type is introduced. A very dry area allows the fire to spread. We can prevent our souls from being dry or experiencing a drought by submitting our lives to God, and regularly giving the living water of the Holy Spirit to our spirits through prayer and the Word of God.

In 2 Samuel 11, King David gave in to the lust burning in his heart for Bathsheba after he saw her taking a bath. His lust resulted in adultery, fornication, illegitimate pregnancy, and the murder of Bathsheba's husband to cover up his sin.

Our eyes can provide light for our Spirits or bring darkness to our souls. They feed our Spirits or feed our souls.

> "Your eye is like a lamp that provides light for your body. When your eye is healthy, your whole body is filled with light. But when your eye is unhealthy, your whole body is filled with darkness. And if the light you think you have is actually darkness, how deep that darkness is!" (Matthew 6:22–23 NLT)

Seeds are planted in your mind when you look at or watch things that are impure or tempting. Once a seed is planted, if it is left to fester, you might be tempted to act on it. Make a covenant with your eyes as Job did. Lust not for the things of this world but set your eyes upon that which is pure, holy, and righteous, flooding your spirit with light. The more you give what you have to God, the more you will experience Him. God will show up!

EAR GATE

> "Pay close attention to what you hear. The closer you listen, the more understanding you will be given—and you will receive even more. To those who listen to my teaching, more understanding will be given. But for those who are not listening, even what little understanding they have will be taken away from them." (Mark 4:24–25 NLT)

We are affected by what we hear, whether good or bad. Some words bring growth and transformation. Other things we listen to can bring doubt, anxiety, fear, or sadness. Satan will be a condemning voice in your mind. He will tell you that you are not good enough. He will say things like, "You've sinned too much. God cannot love you. You're worthless." These are all lies. You may have been verbally abused as a child, and from an early age began to agree with the words spoken over you. Choose to believe the report of the Lord and what He says about you. A plant will wither and die if it is not properly fed. The same applies to God seeds planted in our spirits; if they are not properly fed they will begin to dry up.

Jesus tells us in Mark 4:24–25 to pay close attention to what we hear. Why? There are two reasons. First, we gain life by listening to Him. The more we listen (pay attention to) to His teaching, the more understanding will be given to us.

> "They are not just idle words for you—they are your life. By them you will live long." (Deuteronomy 32:47 NIV)

Second, when we listen to the words, the advice, the counsel of the world, the spiritual understanding that we have from the Holy Spirit will be taken away. How can this be? Imagine you decide to eat whatever you want every day of the week. Once a week you work out for one hour and you believe this one hour a week will balance out all the unhealthy food you have taken in. What little benefit you did for your body during that one hour is taken away by all the unhealthy food taken in during the week. The same is true for the Word of God; if we take in His Word for one hour, one day a week without actively adding to that word daily, what was given will be taken away when it is drowned out by all the worldly distractions, desires, and counsel. This includes secular music, gossip, slander, foul language, crude jokes, and teachings or counsel that are not biblical.

> Wrongdoers eagerly listen to gossip; liars pay close attention to slander. (Proverbs 17:4 NKJV)

MOUTH GATE

Complaining and negative talk are open doors. In the past, when I would be upset, I would repeatedly complain to friends. Things would eventually get better, but only after some time had passed. Then soon enough, another terrible thing would happen. It took me years to discover that I was allowing Satan right into my life. I was creating and inviting havoc because of all the complaining I was doing. Soon I began to speak the opposite of what was happening.

> God, who gives life to the dead and calls those things which do not exist as though they did. (Romans 4:17 NKJV)

I quit complaining about situations to people and closed the access I gave the enemy by repenting to God for the lack of control of my mouth and emotions. I stopped talking about things and began declaring God's word over the situations. This was difficult to train myself to do at first, but the more I did it, the easier it became because I saw how quickly my circumstances changed. I saw the blessings from God for my obedience to His Word.

> Guard the doors of your mouth. (Micah 7:5 NKJV)

> May the words of my mouth and the meditation of my heart be pleasing to you, O Lord, my rock and my redeemer. (Psalm 19:14 NKJV)

We can speak encouraging words, trusting God to settle any of the injustices done against us, or we can speak from our emotions when we become offended and hurt. "Sticks and stones may break my bones, but words will never hurt me." This childhood rhyme is deceptive. Despite the number of times I said it, it never held true. A broken bone is almost better than the brokenness we feel in our hearts when hurtful words are spoken against us. A broken bone will heal in a couple of months. An afflicted heart can hurt for many years and sometimes a lifetime.

> Let your conversation be gracious and attractive so that you will have the right response for everyone. (Colossians 4:6 NLT)

> A gentle answer deflects anger, but harsh words make tempers flare. (Proverbs 15:1 NLT)

Our words can also open the door for God to pour forth into our lives. As we follow in the Way that God has lain before us, speaking what is honest, good, and true, what we declare in our own life will be established. Declare simply means to announce.

> You will also declare a thing and it will be established for you; so light will shine on your ways. (Job 22:28 NKJV)

> And since we have the same spirit of faith, according to what is written, "I believed and therefore I spoke," we also believe and therefore speak. (2 Corinthians 4:13 NKJV)

In our culture, we hear that based on the First Amendment of the United States Constitution, we have a right to be heard, and therefore, say whatever we please. This is not God's way. We must be careful with what we say to others, and at times, not speak at all.

> [There is] a time to be quiet and a time to speak. (Ecclesiastes 3:7 NLT)

> He who has knowledge restrains and is careful with his words, and a man of understanding and wisdom has a cool spirit (self-control, an even temper). (Proverbs 17:27 AMP)

The born-again Christian who is living a life laid down in submission to Christ does not need to fear being demonized. Yes, some days we struggle, but we do not need to fear. The grace of God covers us as we learn and grow more in the image and likeness of Christ. God knows if we truly have a repentant heart and desire to please Him.

Chapter 8

SHUT THE DOOR, BREAK THE CURSE

Any current sin must be removed from a person's life. This will shut the door to the enemy. If the sin is not removed, it leaves a legal right for the enemy to stay. Imagine you have unknowingly let a robber enter your home because you left a door unlocked. When you noticed the door was not secure, you locked it, however the robber is still in your house. He entered because of your open door but you are unaware that he came in. Instead of checking your house, you go on trying to live life as usual. Meanwhile, this person is tormenting you as you try to sleep at night, stealing from you, killing your joy, whispering words of doubt and criticisms, and causing fear, anxiety, oppression, and depression. You cannot figure out why these things are happening to you. To discover the problem, you would need to check your house, find the tormentor, and command him or her to leave. I know this sounds like a silly scenario, but my point is, if someone is not welcome in your house, you would certainly tell him or her to leave. The same applies when spiritual doors have been opened for demons to enter. We must revoke their access, break the curse, and officially cancel their access in our lives.

A common legal right for many is unforgiveness. Forgive, forgive, forgive. One of the most difficult things to do is to forgive someone who has wronged us. When we choose to not forgive someone, it not only steals precious moments of peace and joy but it separates us from God.

> "But if you refuse to forgive others, your Father will not forgive your sins." (Matthew 6:15 NLT)

Holding onto unforgiveness can cause us to not receive the grace from God that He gives us when we mess up. We choose to love others because Jesus first loved us. He showed us how to love others, and how to love our enemies. Jesus, the Son of God, the King of Kings and Lord of Lords was hated, rejected, slandered, beaten, and betrayed by His friends, yet He forgave and asked His Father to forgive them too. If the Son of God forgave all that was done against Him, how much more should we forgive? Early in my spiritual walk I used to ask God why I had to forgive the person(s) who stabbed me in the back. After all, couldn't He look down from His heavenly throne and see how many times I had been mistreated? It did not seem fair. But then He said to me, "How many times did you mistreat Me and I forgave you?"

Forgiving someone is *not* saying, "What you did is okay." What we are actually saying is, "I'm not going to allow you to hurt me anymore by continuously thinking about what you did. I will no longer relive what you did, and experience that pain all over again. I will not let you steal anymore joy and peace. I will not waste any more time thinking about what I cannot change. I am placing my hurt in the hands of God. My trouble is heavy, but His burden is light"

Forgiveness is a consistent mindset. *Merriam-Webster* defines *consistent* as "marked by harmony, regularity, or steady continuity: free from variation or contradiction."[6] We can walk about daily with an immovable determination to resolve any internal conflict

[6] *Merriam-Webster.com Dictionary*, s.v. "consistent," accessed December 13, 2021, https://www.merriam-webster.com/dictionary/consistent.

that may arise due to someone's hostility towards us. Do not be swayed by your feelings. When I am having a hard time truly forgiving someone, I humbly say to Father, "I forgive him or her." Then I confess, "Help me to forgive, Lord. I am having a difficult time. Help me to align my heart with my desire to forgive."

RENOUNCE AND BREAK THE CURSE

If you or your family has any history of trauma, false idol worship, witchcraft, demonic activity, any type of oath or vow, or have been involved in anything else that is forbidden by God, that activity must be renounced, and the curse broken.

> "But I say, do not make any vows! Do not say, 'By heaven!' because heaven is God's throne. And do not say, 'By the earth!' because the earth is his footstool. And do not say, 'By Jerusalem!' for Jerusalem is the city of the great King. Do not even say, 'By my head!' for you can't turn one hair white or black. Just say a simple, 'Yes, I will,' or 'No, I won't.' Anything beyond this is from the evil one." (Matthew 5:34–37 NLT)

Renouncing means declaring you are no longer associated with that activity. Curse-breaking is breaking the curse that came through that activity.

> If a man makes a vow to the Lord, or swears an oath to bind himself by some agreement, he shall not break his word; he shall do according to all that proceeds out of his mouth. (Numbers 30:2 NKJV)

If a vow or oath is made to Satan through ungodly activities, you have bound yourself to him and that vow or oath must be broken. To officially break any legal rights of demons to dwell in you, even if you are unsure of any family history, say this curse-breaking prayer:

> Father, I come before You in all humility and repent of my sins and the sins of my ancestors and of the curses that have been brought on my life. I ask that all the sins and curses on both sides of my family, including my spouse's, be forgiven, broken and put under the blood of Jesus Christ of Nazareth, all the way back through our bloodlines to Adam and Eve. I break all curses on me and future generations. In the name of Jesus, I renounce and break all curses that are on me and future generations associated with false religion, New Age, witchcraft, evil curses, work curses, idle words, divination, false worship, rejection, anger, unforgiveness, fear, depression, condemnation, lust, perversion, rebellion, murder, and child sacrifice. I renounce and break the curses of all ungodly oaths, vows, and dedications that came through my family line all the back to Adam and Eve, on me and future generations. I renounce and break the curse of every ungodly, unholy past and present relationship and soul ties. I declare all these demonic assignments broken, in Jesus's name. Amen.

These are only a few areas where demons can enter, or curses come through. If there is something specific not listed, you can say this prayer and add the specific sin to the list.

> When the seventy-two disciples returned, they joyfully reported to [Jesus], "Lord, even the demons obey us when we use Your name!" (Luke 10:17 NLT)

> "Look, I have given you authority over all the power of the enemy, and you can walk among snakes and scorpions and crush them. Nothing will injure you." (Luke 10:19 NLT)

If you experienced a rapid heartbeat, a tightening in your throat, pain in your head, or pain in any other part of your body while renouncing and curse-breaking, you might need deliverance. Find a deliverance minister near you to pray for you and command any unclean spirits to leave you and go to the pit. If you have a friend who operates in his or her authority given through Jesus, he or she can pray for you as well. Demons must be told to leave, or they will stay.

> But Jesus rebuked him, saying, "Be quiet, and come out of him!" And when the demon had thrown him in their midst, it came out of him and did not hurt him. Then they were all amazed and spoke among themselves, saying, "What a word this is! For with authority and power He commands the unclean spirits, and they come out." And the report about Him went out into every place in the surrounding region. (Luke 4:35–37 NKJV)

When you accept Jesus as your Lord and Savior, you automatically have authority over demons. You must believe it and stand firm on this truth.

Because God's children are human beings—made of flesh and blood—the Son [Jesus] also became flesh and blood. For only as a human being could He die, and only by dying could He break the power of the devil, who had the power of death. Only in this way could He set free all who have lived their lives as slaves to the fear of dying. (Hebrews 2:14–15 NLT)

"These miraculous signs will accompany those who believe: They will cast out demons in my name, and they will speak in new languages." (Mark 16:17NLT)

Chapter 9

TWO COMMANDMENTS

> "Teacher, which is the great commandment in the law?" Jesus said to him, "You shall love the Lord your God with all your heart, with all your soul, and with all your mind. This is the first and great commandment." (Matthew 22:36–38 NKJV)

Have you ever wondered why the first and greatest commandment is to love God with all our hearts, souls, and minds? At one time I would have answered and said, "Because He is God! The Creator of the universe! No one should be above Him!" But the answer is deeper. As a believer, the very core of our being is founded in Him. Our old crumbly walls built on the foundation of the world must be torn down and rebuilt on the Word of God.

> "Therefore whoever hears these sayings of Mine, and does them, I will liken him to a wise man who built his house on the rock: and the rain descended, the floods came, and the winds blew and beat on that house; and it did not fall, for it was founded on the rock. (Matthew 7:24–25 NKJV)

> All ate the same spiritual food, and all drank the same spiritual drink. For they drank of that spiritual Rock that followed them, and that Rock was Christ. (1 Corinthians 10:3–4 NKJV)

When the storms of life come our way, when the enemy tries to ambush us, we will not fall because our spiritual houses have been built on Christ. It is through perfecting our walks with God that we are able to love and forgive others. When we fill our spiritual wells with Living Water, we can give some of that water to others. But we must first fill our wells. A well is made by drilling deep into the ground until the water source is hit. Once hit, water shoots up from the ground like a spout. The water is tested and then allowed to run to remove any debris. To dig our spiritual wells, we must dig deep into the Word of God. We must set time apart for Him, praying, praising, worshiping, thanking, reading, and studying the Word. This is how we tear down our old houses and build the new. We must tear down old mindsets, replacing them with the truth of the Word. Soon you will hit a place where that Living Water from the Holy Spirit will shoot up and as it continues to flow, all the unhealthy thoughts and emotions (debris) will flush out. You can give a taste of this water to another and pray he or she would desire to dig his or her own well.

ALL YOUR HEART (ALL VERSES NKJV)

> Keep your heart with all diligence, For out of it spring the issues of life. Proverbs 4:23. Counsel in the heart of man is like deep water, But a man of understanding will draw it out. (Proverbs 20:5)

> Arise, cry out in the night, at the beginning of the watches; Pour out your heart like water before the face of the Lord. (Lamentations 2:19)

> "A good man out of the good treasure of his heart brings forth good things, and an evil man out of the evil treasure brings forth evil things." (Matthew 12:35)

ALL YOUR SOUL

By the washing of the Word, He shall convert our souls to be manifestations of the glory of God. When others look at us, our lives should be reflections of Christ. This is a work in progress where the grace of God covers us as we grow in Him.

> The law of the Lord is perfect, converting the soul; The testimony of the Lord is sure, making wise the simple. (Psalm 19:7)

> O my soul, you have said to the Lord, "You are my Lord, My goodness is nothing apart from You." (Psalm 16:2)

> The Lord redeems the soul of His servants, And none of those who trust in Him shall be condemned. (Psalm 34:22)

ALL YOUR MIND

We must restore the freshness of His word in our minds every day, making His perfect truth our dominant thoughts, leaving no room for the enemy to deceive or condemn us.

> When doubts [fill] my mind, your comfort [gives] me renewed hope and cheer. (Psalms 94:19 NLT)
>
> You will keep him in perfect peace, Whose mind is stayed on You, Because he trusts in You. (Isaiah 26:3 NKJV)
>
> And do not be conformed to this world, but be transformed by the renewing of your mind, that you may prove what is that good and acceptable and perfect will of God. (Romans 12:2 NKJV)
>
> Set your mind on things above, not on things on the earth. (Colossians 3:2 NKJV)

ALL YOUR STRENGTH

In the Gospel of Mark, "all your strength" is added, emphasizing that with everything we have within us, we should love God. I have a mental picture of a soldier crawling on the ground, weak, exhausted, near death from fighting the battle. But even in this, with the last bit of strength he has, he squeezes out his last words, "For Your glory God. My life is yours." Then he dies.

> You therefore, my son, be strong in the grace that is in Christ Jesus. And the things that you have heard from me among many witnesses, commit

> these to faithful men who will be able to teach others also. You therefore must endure hardship as a good soldier of Jesus Christ. (2 Timothy 2:1–3 NKJV)

> And they overcame him by the blood of the Lamb and by the word of their testimony, and they did not love their lives to the death. (Revelation 12:11 NKJV)

THE SECOND COMMANDMENT

> "And the second, like it, is this: 'You shall love your neighbor as yourself.' There is no other commandment greater than these." (Mark 12:31 NKJV)

I believe as the body of Christ, we flip the first and second commandments around. We try to love others first before we have established ourselves in God's love. The intent of our hearts without God is selfish and evil.

> The heart is deceitful above all things, and desperately wicked; Who can know it? (Jeremiah 17:9 NKJV)

To love others as ourselves, we have to put on God so that the love that others are receiving from us is not our own selfish love but the love of God. To God be the glory!

Chapter 10

THE REST OF MY TESTIMONY

Finally, I had the key to freedom. Depression was about to be out the door, no longer a part of my life. In that pivotal moment when I called out to the Lord from my bathroom floor, He led me to that one book on my bookshelf, *Victory Over the Darkness* by Neil T. Anderson. After I picked the book up and began reading a few pages, my eyes were suddenly opened. Satan was trying to crush me. He was trying to snuff out my life, so I did not live out my life as God had written in my book in heaven. God did not write in my book great sufferings and harm for my life. God authored the book of our lives according to what He had planned, not what we ended up experiencing in this world.

> You saw me before I was born. Every day of my life was recorded in your book. Every moment was laid out before a single day had passed. (Psalm 139:16 NLT)

After I read some of the book, I heard Jesus say, "Don't look to medication for your depression but look to Me." I was at the end of my rope and was ready to do whatever Jesus told me so I could live a much different life. I knew this would be the end of antidepressant medication for me, but I also knew it was going to be a long, hard road. I went through a three-week battle with Satan. I was physically attacked during that whole time. A voice within me said, "If you don't win this fight, you'll never get off that medicine." I was in pain but used scripture to sustain me. At the end of the three weeks, it was over. The pain was gone. I felt physically exhausted. I began to post scripture verses all over my apartment to begin to filter out years of negative thinking and lies. I put them on mirrors, doorways, walls, the refrigerator—everywhere. I constantly listened to teaching CDs and stopped listening to secular music.

Three years passed. I felt better, but something was still missing. I had counseling from both secular and Christian counselors. Still, I found nothing. After another pivotal moment in my life of being fed up with seeking the advice of others, I said to God, "That's it! I am not talking to another counselor! You said the Holy Spirit is our Counselor, so I am going to counsel with Him." Every day after work I took my Bible, journal, worship music, and a blanket to the lake. There I would sit, listen, pray, and meditate on Him as He washed me, cleansed me, refined me. I stopped complaining to others and took all my problems to God. I had a yearning in my heart for Him. The more time I spent with Him, the more that longing grew. I leaned on Him. He comforted me. He loved me the way I needed to be loved—a way that is not possible with people. I encountered Jesus in a way I never had before. When I finally stopped trying to figure it all out, He caused all my problems, emotional and situational, to work out. Everything I was struggling with did not suddenly disappear, but I had peace knowing that He was working on my behalf and in time, they were gone. No longer did I feel alone. Jesus was teaching me just as He had done with others.
(All verses NKJV)

> So the Lord spoke to Moses face to face, as a man speaks to his friend. And he would return to the

> camp, but his servant Joshua the son of Nun, a young man, did not depart from the tabernacle. (Exodus 33:11)

> So he was there with the Lord forty days and forty nights; he neither ate bread nor drank water. And He wrote on the tablets the words of the covenant, the Ten Commandments. (Exodus 34:28)

> So Samuel grew, and the Lord was with him and let none of his words fall to the ground. (1 Samuel 3:19)

> So He Himself often withdrew into the wilderness and prayed. (Luke 5:16)

God desires far greater things for us than anything this world has to offer. He has a plan. He will prepare you for what He is sending you to do. We limit ourselves based on fear, putting faith in our own small abilities instead of the immeasurable ability of God to be able to do anything. Choose today to set aside time dedicated to Jesus and watch God do amazing things in your life. He is calling us up higher, but to get there we have to go down; this means humbling ourselves, dying to our opinions and our ways, and letting Him heal our wounds and wash away the filth of the world that has attached to us over the years. Imagine not taking a bath for ten years and the amount of dirt that would be on you. It would take more than one bath and medical attention to remove the dirt and heal your skin. This is how it is when we come to Christ. He takes our old raggedy clothes and gives us new ones (a new spirit) but the worldly dirt (embedded in our souls) still needs to be washed clean, and our skins (emotional wounds) healed.

> And all who have been united with Christ in baptism have put on Christ, like putting on new clothes. (Galatians 3:27 NLT)

We have years of dirt from hurt, pain, and mindsets that need to be removed so we can stand in the newness of Christ. Spiritually, we are perfect but our souls must be washed by the Word to come into alignment with our spirits. How can Jesus wash it away if we don't give Him the time to do so? How can He train us to do that to which He has called us?

> But first and most importantly seek (aim at, strive after) His kingdom and His righteousness [His way of doing and being right—the attitude and character of God], and all these things will be given to you also. (Matthew 6:33 AMP)

Judas Iscariot, one of the twelve disciples, was taught by Jesus. He heard His words and surely saw miracles performed, yet he turned from Jesus to do something evil, and betray him. How could Judas do such a thing when he sat under the teachings of the Son of God? The answer is he did not have a relationship with Jesus. You can read and study the Bible, but it is through relationship that these words come alive in you, making Jesus more real to you. Imagine you believe you are in a relationship with someone. Instead of spending time with this person, you have only read a book about him or her. You haven't spent time with this person, but you are so excited to tell people about him or her. Meanwhile, this person is waiting to spend intimate time with you, to draw you both closer together, but you just keep reading the book. God is waiting. He is waiting for you to draw closer to Him so He can show you great and wonderful things. When you begin to trust what God says, seeking Him in all sincerity, truth, and righteousness, and putting into action what He has said to do, your life will surely be transformed.

> For the Lord your God is living among you. He is a mighty savior. He will take delight in you with gladness. With His love, He will calm all your fears. He will rejoice over you with joyful songs." (Zephaniah 3:17)

"These things I have spoken to you, that in Me you may have peace. In the world you will have tribulation; but be of good cheer, I have overcome the world." (John 16:33)

References

Beyond Water, "How a water well is built," accessed November 4, 2021, http://www.beyondwater.global/building-a-well/

Centers For Disease Control and Prevention, Health Effects of Secondhand Smoke, last updated January 11, 2017, https://www.cdc.gov/tobacco/data_statistics/fact_sheets/secondhand_smoke/health_effects/index.htm.

Merriam-Webster.com Dictionary, s.v. "ambassador." Accessed April 2, 2019. https://www.merriam-webster.com/dictionary/ambassador.

Merriam-Webster.com Dictionary, s.v. "consistent," accessed December 13, 2021, https://www.merriam-webster.com/dictionary/consistent.

Merriam-Webster.com Dictionary, s.v. "illusion," accessed April 22, 2022, https://www.merriam-webster.com/dictionary/illusion.

Merriam-Webster.com Dictionary, s.v. "transducer," accessed April 22, 2022, https://www.merriam-webster.com/dictionary/transducer.

RAND Corporation. "Psychological Warfare." Accessed April 2, 2019. https://www.rand.org/topics/psychological-warfare.html.

The Bible Gateway, https://biblegateway.com.

Printed in the United States
by Baker & Taylor Publisher Services